D0503787

Cool Schools

by Louise Franklin

NATIONAL GEOGRAPHIC LEARNING | CENGAGE

This is my school.
window
entrance
field
track

I learn the same things that you do.
I learn science, math, and history.

Is this a school?

Yes, it is. It is a school for actors.

Is this a school?
Yes, it is.
screen
simulator

It is a school for pilots. Students at this school learn to fly airplanes.

Students at this school learn to fight wildfires.

They jump from airplanes to fight fires on the ground.

What do students learn at this school?

They learn to make video games.

This kitchen is a school for chefs.
sink
garbage
counter
pot
stove top

The students learn to cook. Yum!

This hospital is a school.
EMERGENCY
flag
sign
flagpole
sidewalk

The students help people who are sick.
They learn to be doctors.

There are many different schools.
What do you want to learn?

architecture

art

music

auto repair